Copyr

ISBN: 9781982912116
Imprint: Independently published

DEDICATION

To my readers, may you find love and peace within yourself. I hope this book brings you smiles on your worst days and brings you happiness in all you strive to accomplish.

ACKNOWLEDGMENTS

To my family, who never fails to support me. Even on my worst days, you have always kept me grounded through every challenge I've ever faced. You have taught me love in it's truest form. You have truly built me into the best person I can be. To my Dad, who made my vision of the front cover come to life.

To my friends, who always keep me going, who never let me settle for anything less than I deserve and who always encourage me to be my best self.

Thank you.
I wrote this book because of all the love you all have brought to my everyday life. Thank you for inspiring me, shaping me, teaching me and loving me in the best way you know how to.

njb

If you're reading this,
welcome back.

My world has gotten
immensely better.
I am doing well,
and feel whole
and happy as ever.

njb

You can either
gawk at the rain
or the sunshine
and let me tell you
when you see
the sunshine,
life gets a lot
brighter.

njb

The most beautiful thing
in the entire world
is a being who feels loved,
happy and whole
after coming up
from such a hard fall.

njb

We all get lost
at some point,
looking in different
directions for the
same damn thing.

Have hope
that you will
find your way,
you'll never get
anywhere with
a bad attitude.

njb

It is never
too late to
begin to
love yourself.

njb

The ones who think
they're damaged
will always feel more.

Once you've
seen darkness,
you start to appreciate
the light.

njb

I wish we were
educated in school
on how to love each other
and ourselves
rather than math
and science that we will
never use in the real world.

njb

Mental note:

To love yourself
is not necessarily
to love every part
of your being,
but to grasp that
you have flaws
and quirks
and you accept them
for what they are.

njb

We bite the apple
from the tree,
and wonder
why we hurt so bad?

njb

Each book
lying on it's shelf,
waiting to be opened,
waiting to be read.

Each of these
books are
a form of
self-help
in whatever way
you need them to be.

njb

Learning how to
be kind to everyone
around you
is the first step
to a happy life.

njb

True strength
lies within
the experiences that
have built you.

njb

If you are
lucky to love
and be loved,
keep it for yourself,
enjoy it,
then share it
with the world
around you.

It's not selfish,
I promise you.

njb

Someday
you will find
what you're
looking for
and if not
you will find
something
much much
better.

njb

I hope someone
picks up this book,
reads these pages,
and feels loved.

Not only loved
but important
in their own skin.

njb

You are the one
that calms me
like the moon,
always being seen
in whichever sky
you're looking up at,
it's always there
as are you.

njb

I picked up my mother's
sewing kit and stitched
up the pieces of myself
that needed fixing.

I bettered myself,
loved myself,
and then I found you.

I came to love you
when you saw the
loose strings and
torn apart stitches
and still loved me anyways.

njb

You see, at first, I did regret you. Being with you, letting you in on the some of the best parts of me, giving you the satisfaction of getting me back in the blink of an eye. But now, that I'm grown and better, I'm so thankful. You taught me there is nothing wrong with showing a man how crazy about him you are, he was just incapable of receiving it. You taught me my worth. That I shouldn't lose a second of sleep crying over something that was never even my fault to begin with. But leaving you was when I learned how to truly love myself. I know what I deserve now.

So thank you for leaving me— I met myself in the struggle and found myself. Some doors need to close for others to open. Don't question it. Just let it happen.

njb

There is nothing
more lovely than
watching a human being
grow.

Grow into love,
grow into success,
grow from the challenges
that have shaped them.

Once believing that you
couldn't and life showing you,
yes,
yes you can.

njb

Life's greatest adventure
came to me, after I got over
my fears and just lived.

njb

You don't always
get what you give.

njb

Water her soul
with adventure,
and be the sunshine
she's always needed.

Some people have
only pricked her thorns,
but not loved her entirely
as they should've.

She will grow to
love you as time passes.

Be patient,
let her bloom on
her own first.

njb

Let's get lost
in the night
and
let the stars
guide us home.

njb

Bloom where you
feel most alive.

njb

Happiness looks
so nice on you.

njb

Radiant beams
of sunlight
glistened upon
his face,
it was hard
not to get
lost in.

njb

Cry with someone.
It's more healing
than crying alone.

njb

Enjoy *you* time.
Having time for
yourself is needed
to learn how to love
and find what
loves you.

njb

No matter what
you are thinking now,
just wait,
sooner or later
you will realize,
your mama
is always right.

njb

Everyone has a plethora
of secrets they don't reveal
to anyone.

A mental illness,
a dreadful past,
something
that keeps them
up late at night.

Consider yourself lucky
if someone opens up
to you,
not everyone
is given the chance,
so listen.

njb

Every time someone
breaks your heart,
it'll feel like your last
day living.
I promise,
it isn't.

You are so
much stronger
than that.

njb

Never wish away time,
you will never live
this exact day again.
Treasure it for
what it is.

njb

Don't blame yourself
for no longer being
friends with the people
you used to be friends
with.

People change like
seasons as do you.

njb

Be with someone
who isn't afraid
of *fear.*

njb

Good
hearts
can
break
too.

njb

You can either
sink with the
thoughts that
flood your mind,
or swim with
those who
are also
struggling to
float around you.

To know
they are there
helps too.

njb

I wish everyone
could see people
through my eyes.

Everyone has a
smile that's waiting
to be cracked.

Everyone has eyes
that tell a life story,
a life story
that may change
your life
forever.

Reach out to
those around
you,
you never know
who you may find.

njb

Depression will submerge
itself into your life
without asking if it's okay,
without asking if *you* are okay.

It will take over like bees
swarming a hive,
anatomizing it's every sector.

It will take all of your sweet,
and turn it from lovely to bitter
leaving you with holes
every which way.

But don't let it ambush you.
You're much better
than you let yourself
believe when you lay
your head down
each night.

njb

You are the reason
I learned to stand alone,
the reason I started
to believe in myself
and
the reason I am here
today.

Thank you.

njb

I am so lucky
to be living
my best life.

njb

I have been taught
a love, that people
write novels about.
And for that,
I am blessed.

njb

I saved you
a seat
on top of
the world.

I've been waiting
for you
to forgive
yourself
and learn
how to
live
a life
filled
with
love.

njb

So happy to find myself
after being lost for
far too long.

njb

I once said to a friend
who was trying to decipher
if the boy she loved
loved her back,

I know it's hard to
put your world in
someone else's hands.
So in that case,
make sure you're happy
with you, rely on you.
But love with all
your heart and don't
be intimidated by fear.
It will only stop you
from making your
best days come
to life.

njb

My parents always
tried to protect me
from a world I was
bound to see.

njb

It's this books job
to sit here
in your dresser drawer,
your bookshelf,
your backpack,
your desk.

It's this books job
to sit here waiting
for you,
arms open
waiting for you
to accept yourself,
and come home.

njb

Life is one
big adventure
&
I'm so excited
to live it everyday.

njb

You are made
with so much
love that
brought you
here today.

njb

I always found
those who
were quiet,
with their noses
in novels
at a coffee
shop,
more interesting
than the boy
next door
twiddling his
thumbs to his
phone.

njb

Be the happy
you never
thought you'd
be.

njb

We talked for
hours on the blue
velvet couch
that
soaked up
all our secrets.

njb

So many voices
must fill that
delicate mind.

Don't let
them tear
you apart.

njb

The world is made
up of way too many
girls who don't feel
pretty,
with a heart once
shattered,
broken
and
bruised
by a boy who
didn't deserve her.

njb

You have
flowers
growing in
your lungs
and
petals
blossoming
through your
heart,

you are
truly
happy.

njb

Blessed with the companions
God has given me to live this
life with and not let me fall.

njb

There is a difference
between someone
who loves you
and
someone who
loves having you.

njb

You've got to love yourself.
You've got to stop on the side of the
road to get the sunset photo
you've always wanted.
You have to take that penny
for good luck you found on
the cream colored pavement.
You have to sit in silence to realize
the beauty of it.
You have to sleep in on Saturdays
and wake up early on Sundays for church.
You have to remind yourself
that just cause the girl next to
you in math class has long blonde
hair and exquisite blue eyes,
doesn't take away from
your being at all.

You're beautiful,
you're kind,
you're special.
You are worth remembering.
& everyone should know this.

njb

Be with someone
who gives you
energy to wake
up in the morning,
not someone who
drains it from you like
the darkness from
the night sky.

njb

By the time that
I finally had enough,
my mind could no longer
take it.

I held the not so good
memories that
laid upon us in the palms
of my hands.
So that each time you
came back I could show
you.
Show you how
it didn't work, and it
truly wasn't meant to.
Starting again wouldn't
suffice that. It wouldn't
change my mind this
time.

Some pieces will never
fit. You must understand
that.

njb

You're
sweeter
than
my
solitude.

njb

The water is rising
up to our knees,
we are drowning
in broken promises
and over anticipated
plans.

My head feels heavy
and this *love* is wearing
me down.

Some things just don't
work out the way we
thought they would.
And when the room
begins to flood,
we both know what's
coming next.

Just remember,
everything happens
for a reason.

njb

I always hold
the most chaotic
parts of myself close.

I hold them tight,
because in those
versions of myself,
I found
strength,
as my wounds
started to bind
back up
and
I began to feel
happy.

njb

Madness may take over
in making you feel
like you don't matter,
but you do,
you always do.

njb

Something you must
accept as I had to come
to accept as well,
you cannot save everyone.

I am someone who
fights to the end
of the earth
to keep a promise,
to be there for someone.

Yet they won't
allow any
room for your
help, they won't allow
any room for you
at all.

You cannot rescue everyone,
so don't lose yourself
in trying to do so.

njb

Time is not the only thing
that heals all wounds.

Coffee shops and midnight talks
with those who continue
to love you at your worst,
keeping busy and allowing
space for yourself,
learning to stand alone on your own
in a crowd full of judging faces,
growing to love yourself
and enjoy your being
are all things that
can heal your wounds
other than
waiting around
for the next best
thing.

njb

Someone who wakes up
to talk to you at 3 am
just to calm your worries,
someone who will tune in
to the thoughts that
flood your mind,
someone who has
patience with your
anxiousness,
mental breakdowns,
and spurts of tears:
this person is worth
keeping around.

They lay your
world in their hands
and even when
it's messy, they
can still hold you
and say
everything will be okay.

Those are the best
kind of people.

njb

You left the old skeleton of you in my closest
along with some tee shirts and old CDs.
I want to box them up and leave it on your
door step,
 but even that you don't deserve.
Through the littlest bit of you that you gave me
and the sun in me you took away,
I owe you nothing.

njb

You didn't deserve
to know me like you did.
Within days, I became
the ground beneath you,
no longer the air you breathe.

njb

A year ago I was asked
to close my eyes and
picture myself in my happy
place,
for that I didn't have one.

My mind was blank.

Smiles filled the room
around me and I felt defeated.

A year later,
I not only have a happy place
but a happy life.

and I thank God everyday.

njb

As a child I was always told
to let my prince come to me.
But was never told what's in between.
I realized it's finding happiness
within yourself and your purpose
in life, and with that you will
end up where you need to be
and your prince will be there
waiting.

njb

Life is precious
and easy to
get lost in,
but don't lose
who you are
through the waves
of society.

njb

Those who comment on your
appearance before they comment
on your soul, are the ones you
need to watch out for.

njb

Your body is not a territory
for those to come and go.
It is not a battleground
to be stomped on
and torn up.

Have enough
respect for yourself
to walk away from
anything that's not
bringing you growth
and stability.

njb

Never lose yourself
in the mess of someone
else's life.

njb

Bravery should never go unnoticed.
It is the courageousness to be
your utter and complete self,
even if it's not always simple to do so.

njb

Regardless of what the world thinks,
stick to what you think.

It's much better to be a leader,
than a follower of something
you don't even believe in.

njb

A lot of times we are
enraged by others for
not filling the void
that we must fill ourselves.

njb

Free yourself from the mold
of society that stuck to
you like glue.

You are not like the rest,
you are you and no one
can best represent
that but yourself.

njb

Trust that someone will
be there in the peak of
your pain
and if not
and you feel like you
have no one,
this book,
this page,
star it,
mark it,
read it
again
and again
because
you're worth it
and loved.

njb

Hearts are filled with poison
and when they break they burst.
He wrenched it into two,
but overtime I sewed
it back up.

And now I
hold the strings together,
keep the blood boiling
as if it had never been
severed before.

njb

Sometimes you have to be
strong for everyone else,
even when you can't even
be strong
for yourself.

njb

My imagination
is so big and so bright,
sometimes
it's hard to tame.

njb

Do not dwell
on the past
for you are
in a safe place
now and that's
all that matters.

njb

You can't
do everything
on your own.

njb

People say to
"be the you
before you met
the one who
broke you,"
but back then
I didn't know
what I know now
and the challenges
that brought me
here.

They made me
a better lover
and a better friend,
strengthened me
when I was weak.

I wouldn't trade
those moments
for the world,
I was able to
come up from
a lapse,
I never thought
I would.

njb

Celebrate other's
success,
it won't dampen
yours.

njb

Don't give your heart away
to just anyone.

They must be kind and patient
enough to wait for however
long you need to heal
your antecedent wounds.

njb

I know what it feels
like to try for someone
you shouldn't have ever
done anything for.

You could move mountains
for someone
and they won't even climb
halfway for you.

Run from those people,
don't settle because
someone
one day
will move
your mountains,
your oceans,
and every star in the
sky just to make you
smile.

njb

You carry the weight
of the world in that mind.

Stop
and
breathe.

Sit in silence.
It won't be until then
that you realize how
captivating it is.

njb

You don't realize
how much you had
changed for someone
else until you remove
yourself from them
like a knife.

I redressed myself several
times to what he
liked best,
did my hair how he
wanted it
and
I wasted way too many
nights waiting for a
call I never received.

I warped myself
so much for a boy
who is no longer
the air I breathe.

Take this as a lesson,
never change for anyone.

njb

I hope you find
someone who knows
how to love you
at your lowest.

njb

Those who aren't afraid to
tell you they miss you,
tell you what reminds them
of you,
tell you how wonderful you
are,
those are the ones you should
carry on with.

njb

My lungs collapsed
in the heat of fear,
I didn't want to get
up that morning.

The bags under my
eyes told a story of
their own,
my heart was in
hibernation while
my mind was trying
to soak up the last
bit of energy I had
left in me.

Yes, I too, have
suffered through
bad days.
But they get better.
They always get better.

njb

You two will be dancing in the kitchen
to your favorite Jack Johnson song,
he will kiss your forehead
and
spin you around
and
I promise you'll feel like you're
on top of the world,
keep that feeling
some place special.

njb

It's never too late
to become the person
you need to be in
order to be happy.

njb

My dad told me
when I was a little girl,
to always hold my head up
high and not to get caught up
with boys.

Then I fell in love
with a boy who
made my heart dance
and my father's words became
refrigerator magnet letters
scrambling to make sense
of themselves.

njb

Someone had once told me
I was never worth anyone's time.
It was then that I began to love
myself much more,
realizing I was deserving
of so much more than
I was filling my bucket with.

So thank you,
you know who you are.

njb

It's very important
to have girlfriends,
find your girl gang
and stick it to the boys
who left you with
broken hearts.

njb

On my first day
of year seven,
my body will be
untouched by the
one who
opened my doors
without asking.

njb

If you haven't heard
it in awhile
or feel like you have
no one to tell you,
just know,

I'm so proud of you.
You've made it so far.
Don't stop here,
you have so much more
exploring to do.

njb

Scrub the floors of all the hate
that once lived there,
build back up the walls,
furnish your soul with what
it needs to heal.

It's never too late
to start again.

njb

You're looking for yourself
in model magazines,
and make up videos,
in the boy down the road,
and sports teams.

You're looking in all the
wrong places.
You are looking
in everything else but you.

njb

In this world,
we are born so lovely,
but convinced to hate
one another based on
beliefs and color.

It's not fair to
be ridiculed by
the way you look
or the person you
want to marry.

If we lived in
a world, where
everyone showed
compassion with
an open mind
and an open heart,
this world would
be a much happier
place.

njb

Love yourself like you
tried to love him.
Put the effort you
placed in him,
into yourself.

Dissect the parts of your being
you don't understand
like why you remember
the lyrics to certain
songs or why you
like to read books before you
see the movie.

Discover what would make
up your best day and what
makes you the happiest
and do just that.

Explore your deepest secrets
and how you healed from
your worst times.

Why waste your entire life
looking for love in another
when you can find it within
yourself?

njb

Something I think
people need
to be more aware of
is that bridging into a
new relationship, you are
not binding yourself to
that person for the rest
of your life, no.

But your time with them
is special, hold it close
and respect it. Because
no, not even *you* know
what the future holds
but why would you
ever love with half
your heart.

Live fearlessly, and
love with everything
you have.
Amazing things wikk
come from
that.

njb

My mother always has
a way of turning sad truths
into life lessons.

She once told me,
"You can't force
somebody to love you.
No matter how
hard you try."

As difficult as it
was to see,
she was completely
and utterly
correct.

njb

I am a lover.
I have always been,
a lover.

I have explored the
most exquisite parts
of you and loved
every bit of them piece
by piece, even the
parts you loathe.

I will never stop
being a lover,
you can barricade
me out like the shots
she fired at you,
but you will never
burn out my flame.

njb

I read a book once,
that taught me
to embrace what we
have now, and to let
God figure out what
comes later.

In this day and age,
I find it fitting that we
all feel like we need
everything in our lives
figured out.

The truth of the matter
is that we need to breathe,
and appreciate what we
have been blessed with now
and leave the rest to him.

njb

Living fearlessly
is throwing yourself
into the sea on a ship
to sail away without
knowing where you
are going, but hoping
you'll find your
way.

njb

Because only in pain
or happiness
do we find the meaning
in life, never along our way.

njb

The person who broke you
cannot be the person that
heals you.

njb

Not everyone who unpacks
your bags,
who explores your being
and loves every part of you,
will end up staying.

Maybe he came because
he was meant to show
you what real love was,
and how you deserve to
be treated and what you do
deserve now.

But maybe he wasn't
meant to stay and maybe
you are both scared.

But it doesn't help
to sit here and
coming up with your
own answers
to your questions,
it doesn't help
to try to wrap your head
around the why's and what ifs.

So I left my final love letter
on the tombstone you made
of us.
I left it there to sulk.

Hoping maybe with time
you would see it my way
too.

But at this point,
there's nothing I can do.
I've said my peace,
maybe it's what I need.

I can only hope
you find whatever it is
you're looking for
and in the meantime
I will learn to reclaim
the pieces of me
you took with you
on your way out.

njb

You're like a ghost
of the past that haunts
me with the fact that
you're no longer around.

njb

I keep painting
pictures of the
thrill of a life
I want to live.

After all the hurt,
I am now
ready to pick
up my brush.

njb

I'm trying to plant
a garden in a grave
with a tombstone
he already left behind
with his name on it
and a phrase,
"I don't love you anymore."

njb

He is not your home,
you are your own home.

Your strength built
your walls,
and
you are your own.

njb

I used to let you
walk on me,
like I was the
ground beneath
your feet.

But I now
love myself more
than to be your
doormat that you
wipe your shoes on
each day.

njb

Sometimes life
will take you
by the hand
and dance
with you,
throw you down,
and tell you,
you are not
good enough,
but yes,
yes you are.

njb

You were someone
I knew so well,
but could never
figure out.

I never knew
what galaxies
you were
constructing in
your mind.
It left me
curious,
curious
to know more.
 I think
that's how I
got caught up
in you,
even if you
didn't love me,
the waves always
come back to
the shore.

njb

Sweet child,
one day
they will swallow
their pride and realize
their mistakes.

They will realize
you were the
best thing they
ever lost,
whether they
come back
or not,
get out of bed,
pick your feet
up and smile
because you
are far too
beautiful
to let depression
swarm you in.

njb

I don't think
my dad could've
ever been more
disappointed in
someone than
you when you left.

Left his little
girl in the pouring
rain and let her
pour her soul
out to you,
just for you
to take it
when you leave.

njb

We accept love for how we've seen it. Your mama's bedtime stories when you were little, and your dad tucking you into bed at night. Your best friend saving you a seat at lunch, and your teacher nominating you for an award.

Our version of love changes over the years based on how it's shown to us. Whether your mama read your stories or your daddy tucked you in. When you meet a boy who you think changes your world but over time, it's not the same anymore. You will accept that love for what it used to be, not for what it's evolved to now.

Because we were once taught about love being so beautiful, you could never wrap your head around the ugliness of it until it hit you too.

But darling, it is beautiful. You've just been searching for it in all the wrong people.

njb

It's not your
fault that
that one person
was incapable
of loving
someone
so bright
so loyal
so beautiful.

Their loss,
they'll see it
one day too.

njb

Some things
are better
left unsaid.

njb

Rising up from
a cold hard fall
and learning to
love again
reflects so much
strength,
especially because
at one point you
thought you
could never
begin again.

njb

If you want to
fall in love with
the world,
you can't be afraid
to live in it.

njb

I finally ripped
out the sword you
wrenched into
my back.

I stopped
feeling so
much pain
from the
blood trickling
down my spine
and the words
you spelled out
on my back
that said,
you're not worth it.

njb

A love letter
to the one who
is still out there.

Thank you for waiting,
for being patient,
for continuing to search
for me.

I know God's plans
are important,
and the timing is too.

I hope to see you soon.

njb

Just because your last love
didn't fit you like your
favorite tee shirt,
doesn't mean it's not
meant for you.

It means that person wasn't,
not love in itself.

njb

I am not here
to feed off
your hunger,
to replenish
your thirst.

I am not
a toy to
be played
with,

I am a woman.
And that's a statement
of it's own.

njb

She's rare,
she's beautiful,
she was born to fly
and everyone knew it.

But here you are
at the bottom
telling her she's silly
and to get down.

Don't cup her fire,
I promise you'll get burned.

njb

I saw you pass me by,
like a train rushing me
head on,
but you missed my stop.

You didn't even look,
I am not even someone
you recognize anymore.

njb

I made a home out of a human
and it wasn't meant to be.

But that's okay
because I've traveled
from place to place
and
I've finally found a home in myself
and I am happy.

njb

The storm will hit
you head on, you
won't even recall
how you made it
through.

You won't even
know if it's fully
over,
but you will come
out of it different.

Pain does that to
people,
it's not bad
to change into
the being you were
meant to be.

I promise you'll
be a hell of a lot
stronger.

njb

Love is sacred.
Only makes sense that
how you view and love yourself
is what others will pick up on.
Remember that
next time you begin
to resent yourself
for something completely
out of your control.

Love yourself,
it's important.

njb

Despite what mud
your past has
dragged you
through,
you deserve a
wonderful life
filled with
extraordinary
people
in it.

njb

When walking into
the love of another,
you're walking into
a world of change,
and whether or not
this lasts, we are both
going to come out
to be different people.
And I hope it's for the
best.

njb

We take what's temporary
and our minds morph it
into something permanent.

We take plans and construct
a future out of them.
We build our lives off the
people who come and go
and we are forced to make
a home in someone new
while still packing our
stuff up from the last.

Make sure you always
have a safe and comforting home
within yourself.
You'll always have *you*
to go back to.

njb

A person who doesn't
know their worth will
settle for less than they
deserve and dig themselves
in a hole from hell.

They won't be respected
how they should be,
they won't get treated
with the best.

It's not selfish
to set standards.
It's seeing the
worth and value
in yourself and
showing other
people you won't
accept any less.

njb

I began to fear
the best to come
and became afraid
of trying for what I
deserve.

It wasn't until
many people
confronted
me, saying how
strong I am.
How they look
up to me for getting
through so much
and while still having
the brightest smile
 in the room.

How we see ourselves
is often a lower grade
of how others see us.

Find the good in you,
find the flaws,
accept them for what
they are and
fall in love with your
life, just as others do
from a far.

njb

Fate has a way
of circling back
on us,
don't think
just because
you're caught up
in the storm now
that you won't ever
get out.

When the rain
is gone and the
clouds uncover
themselves,
your sun will
shine.

njb

We are on our knees
begging for something
better, but not willing
to wait the time for
the wounds to heal.

njb

We lost the art of loving
because we stopped being
artists of truly seeing people.
We are afraid that if they look
too closely they will find us.

We are just a generation of humans
forgetting how to love.
Burying ourselves under
thick soil beneath the flowers
that grow on us like the people
who come and go in our lives.
Leaving a little bit of water,
filling us up, helping us stand tall
into the big and bright sunflowers
we are today.

Except that's not what we see,
we are so worried about the
unexpected things that hit our
skyscrapers, confusing our
hearts that form to ashes and debris.
We water down the word vulnerability
by letting it slip carelessly out
out of our mouths.
We define relationships through
social media, approval of likes
and too much poise
with not enough rawness.

We are afraid of the bare
and unfiltered parts of us
that are just *too ugly* for
anyone to hold tenderly.

We aren't told that we
are exquisite and beautiful.
So we have women who
cover up their eyes with makeup,
and men who mask their aroma
with cologne.

Because in this world,
we are meant to make a home
out of the people and places
we have been to,
not in the comfort of our
own skin.

njb

He often tells me that he was an accident.
He's by far not an accident,
and I wish I could take the pain
of feeling that away.
Because I once felt that way too.
It gets better,
I promise it gets better.

He is much more than a flower,
much more than the stars.
He is a masterpiece
sold short off the map of life.

Listen my love,
you are no accident to me.
You are my favorite rainy day
and my treasured Sunday morning.
You're much more than the flaws
you entangle in your being.
And if my opinion could change
the way you construct your mind
of such thoughts,
well then boy,
I have a lot more to say.

njb

Even in a day of misunderstandings,
when sadness and bad luck hang
themselves up like frames on a wall,
I still remain smiling.

Someone somewhere can't find
water to drink,
someone somewhere doesn't have
a roof over their head,
someone somewhere doesn't
receive the love I am so lucky
to be flooded with.

And for that, I am grateful.

njb

You found bits of me
that I didn't know existed
and in you I found a love
that I never believed
would find me.

njb

Your eyes have seen so much,
I question how you're still here.
But I thank God that you are.

njb

I have always let the
love of others take
the place of the love
I should've been
filling up myself.

I have told many
this phrase, but
never stuck to
it myself.

Now I know,
have learned
and grown,
that *you must*
love yourself
before you can
love someone else.

njb

You make me wild
and I think that's what
I love about you.

njb

When I was little
someone would tell
me their fears,
and suddenly
I became afraid
of them too.

njb

I took five steps forward
and two steps back
and not that those
steps were filled
with regret
but to reflect on
where I have been
where I am now
and where I'm going.

njb

I once heard this phrase
that stuck with me,
"let people do whatever
the hell they want to do,
so you'll see what
they'd rather do."

Take this as you please.

njb

We drank over
our fears and
threw our cans
at the stars,
saying hell no
to doubts as
we laughed endlessly.

Tonight,
I can almost see a
face on the moon,
and it's smiling
right back at me
spelling out your
name in constellations
because it knows you're
on my mind tonight.

njb

Looking back at past relationships,
right once they let me in
I met ignorance and insecurity
at the door and vulnerability
picked the lock.

They were too afraid to be human
too afraid to stretch out their own skin
from scars that tell us stories
and stretch marks that spurted with age,
too afraid to live life to the fullest,
and from there they would barricade
their own wisdom
to hide the memories,
they could never tell.

I fell in love with too many boys
who underestimated who I would
grow to be.

And then I fell in love with me.

njb

Dear ghosts of the past,

whether us parting ways
was ugly or not.
I hope you take
growth and grace
with you along your way.

And if you were to
reflect on anything
from me,
remember my heart
of gold for the weak spots.

But most of all,
I wish you the best
on this journey you are
embarking on,
called life.

njb

One day I'll marry poetry,
because words on a page
will never hurt me,
they can never go back
on their word.

njb

An important thing to
remember is,
you will learn
more from people
than you ever will
learn in school.

I am taught passion
through the glowed
up eyes of another
and scars that make
up stories of wars
they once fought.
Whether it be overseas,
or a constant battle
with themselves.

You learn a lot
about someone,
by how they
handle things
and how they come
up from them.

You will never
learn this in school.

njb

You still lifted your head on days
that were more unbearable than
this one.

I believe in you.

njb

I think it's important to make peace
with the world, with the things you used
to stumble upon and the people you
come across.

Darling, I am not doubting that things
have wronged you.

But I know I'm at my happiest
when I don't have a worry
in the world.

Life is better this way.

njb

Hang me up like
one of the portraits
on your wall
and hold me
like I'm your
honorary trophy,
show me off like
I'm your brand
new sneakers,
and love me
like you
love your mama.

njb

My best advice I have to
give is if someone
wants to be in your life,
they will make a hell
of an effort to do so.

Whether it be God,
the universe,
whatever you believe
in, they will make sure of it.

So if you lose someone
due to the lack of them
not cherishing you enough,
not understanding what
they had,
or not realizing how
wonderful you truly are,
don't chase them.

They are simply not
worth your time.

njb

I am who I am.
I am what experiences
have made me.
I am what people have
left with me.
I am my parent's
who raised me.
I am happy,
I am loved,
by me
and
having just
that is perfectly
fine with me.

njb

ABOUT THE AUTHOR

Natalie is a student at Grand Valley State University who has been writing since she could hold a pencil. She always loved poetry and resonated with it personally. While going through her life journey, Natalie has encountered some experiences that she believes could not go unwritten. Her first book was published September, 2017, called *Making Homes Out Of Humans*. Her first book focuses on her experiences and how they shaped her, as this one shows how far she has come from those experiences.

Through the bad times, good times, hardships and rough relationships; she finally finds a home in herself, in another and finds happiness once again. She believes this book is a tribute to those who need love and confidence within themselves. She hopes her words speak humbly and help many along the way.

CPSIA information can be obtained
at www.ICGtesting.com
Printed in the USA
BVHW031254190420
577913BV00001B/200